THE CUP
Devotional Series

THE CUP
Devotional Series

VOLUME I
Personal Communion

JON PAUL TUCKER

The Cup
ISBN: 0-88144-419-7
Copyright © 2009 by Jon Paul Tucker

Published by
THORNCROWN
A division of Yorkshire Publishing Group
9731 East 54th Street
Tulsa, OK 74146
www.yorkshirepublishing.com

CONTENTS

THE THIRD QUARTER
Keep Pursuing God

THE FOURTH QUARTER
PASSION FOR HIS PRESENCE

Acknowledgments

It is so important to me to thank those who have had a part in The Cup this past year. You may not have had a direct hand in writing this book but it is your ideas and faith that have sparked every last word. Again and again I find myself inspired, encouraged and strengthened by The Cup. It is exciting, and a true blessing, to know this is only the beginning. There will be so much more to come out of this amazing journey.

I thank all of you, and you know who you are. May God bless each and every one of you, family and friends. I love you all and I hope this devotion speaks volumes to your heart and life.

And Father, thank you for your work in me.

Complete in Him,
Jon Paul Tucker

Introduction

THE BEGINNING

On February 14th, 2008 I woke up early around 4:30 a.m. rolled out of bed to enter into the living room for my daily devotional. But this morning was unique because I felt for the first time ever a need to receive communion. Why? Well, the sense and urge to do this was brought on by an idea I had been working on since November 2007.

The idea was to distribute communion juice to local Church's for the purpose of raising funds for a camp. It all began one day with a thought after a cousin visiting from Michigan said to me as they were leaving "I won't commune with you until I see you again." It reminded me of a statement Jesus made to his disciples along the same line in Matthew 26:29 "I tell you, I will not drink of this fruit of the vine from now on until that day when I drink it anew with you in my Father's kingdom." NIV And so like Mary I pondered all these things in my heart.

Since I sat on a local rural water district board with a man who had a winery I thought I would ask him about communion juice. He said it was all a matter of marketing, the exact thought I had already had. With no degree in marketing I set out on a quest to discover there isn't a lot of companies trying to promote or sell communion juice. Someone has already captured the market with a common household name when you think about Concord grape juice. And it seems every Church uses this less than expensive brand. But I found through my connections a great tasting locally grown Concord grape juice. Though it was ten times the cost and came in a wine bottle I created a label and introduced it to my wife and then my brother. It seemed perfect.

But this morning I was challenged to embark on a journey of faith, doctrine and tradition that had long been practiced in every Church around the world. Only this time I was receiving communion with no Pastor or Priest just God and myself. The experience was eye opening and heart transforming. What I discovered would change my outlook on communion forever. With great joy I got up went to my computer got online and formed an L.L.C. called First Light Distributing. It was a name that had its own true story from the past November. And so here I was excited about something I knew little about, personal communion.

This isn't taught in Sunday school so you must understand what I am dealing with. This is a Holy sacrament and an everlasting ordinance set forth by God thousands of years ago. What was I thinking and doing? One thing certain I was ready to have the experience again. And so the next day, week and into the months I went receiving personal communion and administering communion to my family as well. The discovery was that communion is "always personal" if you are alone or in a crowd of five thousand.

A few days after this event my brother called and began to tell me he was taking communion and that he was planning to take it for the next forty days. Great! I was doing the same thing. He had the idea of receiving communion for forty days instead of giving something up for lent. From that came the idea for a forty-day devotional centered on personal communion. The revelation began to flow and I began to write, not so much about communion but just about all the things in my heart on the word of God.

Now almost a year later I am still taking communion regularly and the experience is still as sweet as ever. The good news is that was the way the Lord intended it to be for us. Fresh and new just like the new fallen dew of an early spring morning. Some days His presence is overwhelming, as the Holy Spirit seems to permeate the room. Other days it is just experiencing the knowledge of the body and blood, what he has done, what he is doing and what he will do. No matter what the experience we don't always want to go by our feelings it must be deeply rooted in the word and our faith. Romans 1:17 "For in the gospel a righteousness from God is revealed, a righteousness that is by faith from first to last, just as it is written: "The righteous will live by faith." So by faith I receive the cup and realize it is always enough to fill me up and bless me.

What Communion really means to me

Communion in its purist form is intimate fellowship with God. This is a bear all experience with you and the Creator of the universe. Intimacy is a part of relationship we all long for. In the Garden of Eden is where intimate fellowship began with Adam and Eve. The day they allowed sin to enter in that intimacy was broken. They realized their own nakedness and were ashamed for God to see them. Though intimate fellowship was broken God continued to talk to them but from a distance. God is still speaking today to many but from a distance. Not because he is choosing it to be that way but we won't allow Him any closer.

Recently God spoke a word into my heart and said "The seeds of intimacy are the Divine Inspiration that give birth to the Manifestation of God's Glory." God desires intimate fellowship with us so that the seed, his word, in us can bring forth Glory to His name through our lives. The best demonstration God has to show people His Glory is you and I. His creation has been showing His Glory since the beginning of time but men still refuse to see it. So it is time for Glory to be birth in the inner sanctuary of our heart where God exist to bring forth His Glorious Light so the world can know Him intimately.

It is the person of the Holy Spirit that works in us that will bring this Glory to life. He is the presence we will experience in communion. Jesus sent the Holy Spirit to help us, guide us and to teach us all things. It is the Holy Spirit that will germinate the seed inside you and cause it to grow. The same Holy Spirit that convicts of sin also opens the eyes of our understanding so that we can both know and understand him. Remember after the Last Supper Jesus began to teach his disciples of his intimate relationship with his Father. It was then that the disciples began to both see and understand what He was saying. Communion can open our eyes through the Holy Spirit and reveal God's word more clearly to us. After all the word is his "New Covenant" for us to live by.

Listen to what I am about to tell you this is what "I believe" about communion. This is not what I have been taught but what I have learned through this experience. No one has cornered the market on this subject. There are many different ways in which to receive communion. Personal Communion is the first one for me so remember it is "always personal." Those who view communion as a sacrament to only be done in a body of believers may challenge you if you choose to participate in personal communion. The second is "Family Communion" that to me stems back to the beginning. When God instituted the family it was for them to have communion one with another. The ordinance of "Passover" was for each individual family to participate. This was a true foreshadowing of Communion and the work Christ would do on the Cross. And then the third is of course "The Communion of Saints" or the body of believers when we gather. All three of these experiences and expressions of our faith are vitally important and central to our faith.

Communion should not be an afterthought of our worship but a central foundation of our faith in Him. When the evangelical Church gets a hold on the pure meaning of communion look out! Revival fires will be lit, because it is all about the body and blood of our Lord and Savior Jesus Christ! Without it where would we be and what would be the meaning of the Church. It would be a dead and powerless religion. But because of it we can overcome by the blood of the lamb and the word of our testimony! Amen.

WHAT COMMUNION CAN BRING

First and foremost we must recognize what Paul taught us about communion. This to me is a right of passage that is only offered to those who believe in and on the name of Jesus Christ and trust him as Lord and Savior. Without the shedding of blood there is no forgiveness of sins. Someone had to die for us and there was only one worthy who led a life without sin and he was and still is the Son of God. In I Corinthians 11:23-26 Paul lays out what the Lord had revealed to him to tell other believers about. Communion brings revelation of Christ through his body and blood. Our eyes are open to realize salvation comes from God alone when we participate in this meal.

This meal heals us spiritually, physically and emotionally when we receive it in faith believing that all Christ did through the work on the Cross is complete. Also we must examine ourselves before the meal or none of this will take place according to I Corinthians 11:27-32. This meal is complete and lacks nothing to sustain us it represents the word, bread and the Spirit, the wine. For us to commune with God his Spirit must live within us and we will need his word daily to sustain us. The word and Spirit are always in agreement with the New Covenant God has made with us. Communion brings us into remembrance of complete Salvation.

Communion brings the inner ear of our heart closer to listening to the Spirits voice that longs to teach us, guide us into truth and liberate our lives. Communion is a celebration of the life we now live by faith in the Son of God. No wonder the early Church did it daily. They were reminded time and time again how good he really is. And that every promise he made to them would come to pass in its time. We are still looking for his coming and he said to continue this even as we see the day approaching.

One of the most important element that communion brings is unity. We are one body and through this meal we demonstrate our connection through the body and the blood. This meal can heal relationships between us. Allowing the Holy Spirit to have His way as we examine ourselves it can do nothing but bring us into unity with him. How can we say we love God if we hate our brother? This meal challenges us to examine every area of our live and especially our relationships. That is what communion is all about intimate fellowship that only comes through relationship.

So let me recap what communion can bring to the believer first revelation then healing also ears to hear and most importantly unity. I'm sure there is more since you are communing with the triune God of the universe. But these are clearly benefits of daily personal communion.

Once this foundation is set in stone, the corner stone, Jesus Christ, life begins a new chapter. What will become the next lines written on the pages of our hearts? What were we created for? Communion with God as we worship him with our whole being and singing praise unto Him. Through this we can discover our true purpose in life.

GOD'S CAD PROGRAM

To every person is given a cup that represents his or her lot in life. Every cup is unique by design and not one is exactly alike. Its creator determines the size, shape and style of that particular cup. Can a cup truly question its creator? God is the Creator, Author and Designer of our lives. That is His CAD program by which you were made. The only question you have to get answered is what is your purpose? The acronym for cup is, Called Unto Purpose. The CAD program is to help you discover that purpose, plan and promise for your life. In pursing that discovery your life will become fulfilled.

In the garden of Gethsemane Jesus was faced with his own cup. He prayed, "My Father, if it is possible, let this cup pass from Me; yet not as I will, but as You will." Matt. 26:39 Again in verse 42 he prayed a second time "My Father, if this cannot pass away unless I drink it, Your will be done." So what should your response be when faced with your cup? The greatest challenge for us is often fear. Fear stands in the way of a life of Faith. Accepting your cup, or purpose, can be the most rewarding moment in your life, and yet somehow fear wants to rob the very blessing God has for you. Even though there is a cross to bear on the other side of your cup, or purpose, Christ's offers you His cup daily to remind you of His purpose so that you will have the courage to live in yours. "Let us fix our eyes on Jesus, the author and perfecter of our faith, who for the joy set before him endured the cross, scorning its shame, and sat down at the right hand of the throne of God." Heb. 12:2 NIV

In the days ahead you have the opportunity to experience first hand the challenge of understanding the CAD program. Every life has a beginning and end but the most important time is in between these two points that will count for eternity. Living in the Light of the Alpha and Omega will help define what your purpose in life is really all about. The question between these two points can only be answered by you, "What will you do with Christ?" After you answer that question the real test begins to receive or reject the cup he has set before you. You will soon realize it's not about you!

For a person to answer "no" to Christ calling is the absolute surety of damnation. To answer "yes" is to engage upon a journey of faith that is unequal to anything we could ever imagine. But without the Creator, Author and Designer of our lives we would be left with nothing to live for. Therefore it is essential to our life to embrace the cup, your purpose, with a grip of faith that says, "my life is not my own." "I have been crucified with Christ and I no longer live, but Christ lives in me. The life I live in the body, I live by faith in the Son of God, who loved me and gave himself for me." Gal. 2:20 NIV "You were bought at a price. Therefore honor God with your body." 1 Cor. 6:20 NIV

How much of your destiny is involved in his design is determined by how much you are willing to pursue him. Your unique design and plan for this life was written and carved out for you long before you came into being. And yet God offers you the opportunity to join in with him on your journey or you can choose to go your own way. The choice is totally yours.

Once you choose the cup remember what Christ had to face. There is a cross before every believer to bear, but we bear it through the grace of our Lord and Savior, Jesus Christ. The acronym for cross is Christ Redemption Offering Sinners Salvation. Through His grace He unveils His purpose, plan and promise for our life. That all leads us to His Covenant. The acronym for covenant is Contract Of Value Effecting Natural And Necessary Things. God placed such great value on his covenant that He gave His son so that you could partake of all its promises and benefits.

God wants to establish His Covenant with you through your cup, purpose in life, and the cross you bear. This becomes an eternal witness to His Kingdom on the earth today. The impact of a significant life is eternal. One word, one moment, one act could change the life of an individual forever! And you could be a part of that when you except your responsibility and take your cup.

The message of the Gospel is Christ shed His blood so that I might live eternally in His light! That starts here on earth when I live daily in the light of His word, Jesus, the Covenant. John 1:1-6. When you except your cup you choose to bear the cup of Christ that sets the captives free and in so doing you find freedom, freedom from self.

Matt. 10:38,39 NIV says, "and anyone who does not take his cross and follow me is not worthy of me. Whoever finds his life will lose it, and whoever loses his life for my sake will find it."

The sin of every man lies in his addiction to his own cup. When you exchange your cup for His cup, life takes on a whole new meaning. Purpose is poured out with a passion to live, really live! Nothing can take the place of the life He gives. The pouring out of your cup into His makes us one! Now you can bear faith, hope and love. Now you can see the CAD program and His Dream. Now you can hear His Spirits call on your life to follow him. Now you can speak with boldness and confidence as one who understands the purpose of Communion with God, experiencing Him and discovering your purpose.

How to Receive Communion

Before you embark on this journey through the cup there are a few simple steps to take in the process. First you must believe and confess Jesus Christ as Lord and Savior of your life in order to take communion, the bread and wine. (Rom. 10:9,10 I Cor. 11:23-27)

The Next step is examination according to I Corinthians 11:28. This examination process starts with your relationship with God. Examine your relationship with others and then examine your outlook on your future. If you feel you have nothing between you and God or others and yourself then you are ready to eat and drink. The body and blood is for our past, present and future. God is concerned how you view all of it.

Now all you need is a piece of bread, a wafer or cracker to represent the body of Christ and Juice to represent the blood of Christ. Turn to I Corinthians 11:23-26 and use this as your guide to receive the bread and wine.

Thank Him for His body that was broken for you and then eat. Thank Him for His blood that was shed for you and then drink. Remember and meditate on the promise of life through His death, burial and resurrection. As often as you do this do it in remembrance of the covenant He has made between us through this.

Every day as you take the challenge of the cup remind yourself it is for my good God did all this. I pray that you will enjoy the fruit of the vine and experience the presence of the Holy Spirit like never before. Remember we will do this with Jesus again in his Kingdom (Matt. 26:29) so we might as well prepare daily for the King.

This is the message of Communion, may it bring faith, hope and love as you experience the presence, power and provision God has for you now!

Jon Paul Tucker

The Cup Challenge

Have you ever longed for a real living experience with God? Are you yearning for his presence continually? Do you have a need to see his power and provision in your life right now? The Cup is God's invitation to a 40-day pouring out of revelation of his presence, power and provision through daily communion. This is your opportunity to experience first hand what the early church practiced daily, breaking bread and celebrating the Lord's Supper. (Acts 2:46,47) This could be a life altering experience that I pray will become the lifestyle of believers. Now the question is are you ready for the challenge? Take the challenge eat the bread and drink the Cup and see what God will do in this humble time of remembrance!

Jon Paul Tucker

"...the Lord Jesus the same night in which he was betrayed took bread:
And when he had given thanks, he brake it, and said, Take, eat: this is my body, which is broken for you: this do in remembrance of me.
After the same manner also he took the cup, when he had supped, saying, This cup is the new testament in my blood: this do ye, as oft as ye drink it, in remembrance of me." I Corinthians 11:23-25 KJV

Ask yourself, does God want to commune daily with me? If yes, how will I become passionate about communing with him?

"A life filled with passion becomes an outpouring of passionate living!"

Prayer: Father God I accept this challenge and desire that as I go through it you will strengthen me so I can find passion for you. Amen

The First Quarter

RESTORE A PLACE OF WORSHIP

Restoration is a process of rebuilding or re-establishing something. Without a proper foundation nothing built can stand. Today I lay before you an opportunity to be restored into fellowship or communication with God which is a foundational way for you to grow. Over the next forty days you are being challenged to worship God by receiving communion and using this devotional as a guide to assist you. Communion is a central act of our worship before God in the Church and your home. Without the shed blood and broken body of Jesus where would you be? When we honor the blood of the Covenant powerful things can happen in your life.

The first thing that you must do to engage in the "cup challenge" is to restore a place of worship in your life. Begin by choosing a place in your home as a place of worship during this process. This could be a spare bedroom, the living room or wherever you feel comfortable in spending time in praise, prayer and receiving communion. This place will become the place for your altar before God. By doing this you have taken the first step of being open to listen to God speak to you over the next 40 days.

In Genesis 8:20 we find the first altar built in scripture was by Noah. Noah was a righteous man and had found favor with God. (Gen.6:8,9) And so God spoke to Him and told him to build an ark for his family and the animals on the earth. He followed the instruction of the Lord and built it just as God had commanded him to. (Gen. 6:22) The interesting thing is that God made a promise to Noah that he would establish his Covenant with him. (Gen. 6:18)

And so the story goes on, the flood came for forty days and forty nights the waters from the deep continued to flood the earth. (Gen. 7:17) God wiped out every living thing except Noah and his family and the animals he had brought into the ark. And the waters flooded the earth for a hundred and fifty days. (Gen. 7:21-24) In chapter 8 the waters began to recede and Noah began looking for a place to land. After many days attempting to find land it finally came and God told Noah to come out of the ark.

Noah was a faithful man all his life and never let go of God's promise of a covenant. In the trial period of his life to obey God and follow his instruction to build the ark he never lost sight of God's promise. In the transition from the trial to hold on through the flood would come the transformation, the Covenant with God. So, the first thing Noah did when he came out of the Ark was build an altar and prepare a burnt sacrifice to God. (Gen. 8:20) It was pleasing to God and he said, "As long as the earth endures, seed-time and harvest, cold and heat, summer and winter, day and night will never cease." Gen. 8:22 "Seed-time and harvest" is still at work today.

In Chapter nine God makes his covenant with Noah and tells him the same thing he told Adam and Eve to "be fruitful and increase in number and fill the earth." God told him other things and then said, as a sign of my covenant, that he would never flood the earth again he put a rainbow in the clouds. This sign still remains today and is a reminder to us of God's faithfulness to his Covenant with man. God continued to make covenants with man and men continued to build altars and make sacrifices to him.

This is essentially what Jesus was emphasizing when asked what the first and greatest commandment was. In short love God with your whole being and so fulfill the first commandment of the law. (Ex. 20:1-6) Without an altar in your life your life is easily altered. Jesus has already made the greatest sacrifice for you and now he invites you to his table to eat and drink. This altar will alter your life!

God must be preeminent in your life. Prioritize your place of worship every day, not as religious duty but as the need for a loving relationship with a God who loves you. As you worship ask the Holy Spirit to fill the room with His presence. Then watch how the order of worship begins to change you in the process. This is your way of having an encounter with God so you can have a living experience through communion or as some call it the Lord's Supper. Your place of worship can be at any time according to the demands of your schedule. Remember God looks at your heart to see what's in the cup not the beauty of the cup! As you restore the place of worship in your life, God will restore worship in your life for God inhabits the praises of his people!

"The most important one," answered Jesus, "is this: 'Hear, O Israel, the Lord our God, the Lord is one. Love the Lord your God with all your heart and with all your soul and with all your mind and with all your strength.'"
Mark 12:29,30 NIV

"Alterations start at the Altar!"

Prayer: Father God, help me build an altar in my heart and home to restore a place of worship as I dedicate the next 40 days to communion with you through this devotion. Holy Spirit I ask you to fill my place of worship with your presence because I confess Jesus as Lord of my life. Amen

Day 1

THE CUP OF EZRA

*On the fourteenth day of the first month, the exiles celebrated
the Passover. Ezra 6:19 NIV*

Restoring a place of worship in your life is the most important place to start. The first and greatest commandment is, "Love the Lord your God with all your heart, soul, mind and strength." (Mk. 12:29,30) This is where it starts, building a place of worship in our lives. Without this you cannot establish the second command to "love our neighbor as ourselves." In a nutshell love God, serve people, worship always precedes ministry. Ezra led the people of Israel back to their homeland and the first thing needed was to build back the temple. This may seem like an easy task but much opposition came. The enemy does not want you to worship God so he will attempt to stop your pursuit of God. But just as the people of Israel were held captive for so long when they returned the first thing needed to be set in order was worship. God orders your steps each day when your priority is to worship him and him alone. Joshua said, "As for me and my house, I will serve the Lord." Surrender your heart to God with humility and build a place of worship in your life. You are the temple of the Holy Spirit and God wants to inhabit you. The first place to start is at the Lord's Table as the Israelites did when they celebrated Passover in Chapter 6 starting in verse 19. Once you build your own place of worship then celebrate it!

Ask yourself, have I built a place of worship in my own life?

As you read and meditate on Ezra, I pray you will restore the place of worship inside your heart today!

"Once you build a place of worship then Celebrate!"

Today's Prayer: Father Thank you for establishing a place of worship in my heart and life today as I receive communion. Amen

INSIGHTS

Day 2

THE CUP OF REPENTANCE

But after Uzziah became powerful, his pride led to his downfall. II Chronicles 26:16 NIV

This verse says nothing about repentance but it is an example and warning to you about sin and especially pride. My Pastor preached on this text one Sunday in 2007 and it caused me to repent at the altar before taking communion. The scripture points out that pride goes before a fall and I was falling but I found a safe place to land, right in the arms of my savior Jesus. It was a true moment of examining my heart before God, just me and him and I knew I needed to repent, turn and go another way, before taking the bread and the wine. The backlash of sin in my life had already caused me enough pain and suffering, it was time to change before the leprosy set in. God is gracious to you today, to allow you the opportunity to repent before it's too late.

The first work of the Holy Spirit is to convict us of our sin. Allow him to do His work in you every day so that you can be more effective in your worship, the word and your witness.

Ask yourself, have I allowed pride or any sin to come into my life in any area?

As you read and meditate on II Chronicles 26 I pray you can realize the need to change and receive his cup of repentance through his kindness today! Romans 2:4

"The point between judgment and promise is Repentance!"

Today's Prayer: Father I repent of my sin before you knowing you cleanse me of all unrighteousness according to I John 1:9. Thank you for your forgiveness present in communion.
Amen

INSIGHTS

Day 3

THE CUP OF SANCTIFICATION

Who have been chosen according to the fore-knowledge of God the Father, through the sanctifying work of the Spirit, for obedience to Jesus Christ and the sprinkling by his blood:
I Peter 1:2 NIV

Sanctification is a powerful word we do not hear very often in the local Church today. Sanctification means it has been set apart for a holy use, or consecrated. Holiness is used often in place of this word. To be Holy and set apart is a hard concept for most of us. You mean me Lord? Yes, he has set you apart from this world for a holy purpose and has sanctified you with the sprinkling of his blood that covers you wholly and completely. Titus 3:5 *NIV* says, "he saved us, not because of righteous things we had done, but because of mercy. He saved us through the washing of rebirth and renewal by the Holy Spirit,"

I recently had the opportunity to participate in a Passover seder at my Church and the first cup of four was the cup of sanctification. We were celebrating what God promised his people, "…I will free you from the forced labor of the Egyptians…" Exodus 6:6. Through the sacrifice of Jesus Christ shedding his blood for you and me we are set apart to worship him alone. The sanctifying work of the Holy Spirit is a continual reminder of that.

Ask yourself, have I set apart and made a holy place of worship for God in my life?

As you read and meditate on sanctification I pray you will sense the sanctifying work of the Holy Spirit in your life today!

"We are sanctified by the washing of His Word!"

Today's Prayer: Father, wash me in your blood and with your word, set me apart for a Holy use as I receive communion. Amen

INSIGHTS

Day 4

THE CUP OF HUMILITY

Do nothing out of selfish ambition or vain conceit, but in humility consider others better than yourself.
Philippians 2:3 NIV

Your attitude should be the same as that of Christ Jesus.
Philippians 2:5 NIV

Humility really is a daily choice on your part in your words, actions and attitude. Treating others with respect becomes a key role in checking your attitude. Those who serve you deserve the same respect as those you serve. True humility comes out of a heart that loves God and loves people and considers others needs over their own. Jesus humbled himself and became obedient to death-even death on a cross for your sake and mine.

Ask yourself, what could Christ do in my life if I would just drink his cup of humility?

God's promise is Grace to the humble! James 4:6.

As you read and meditate on Philippians 2:1-5 I pray that you will find the grace you need to walk in humility today!

"The greatest coat of armor is the cloak of humility"

∽

Today's Prayer: Father God, cloak me in humility today as I walk before you and others. Amen

INSIGHTS

Day 5

THE CUP OF GRACE

But he said to me, my grace is sufficient for you, for my power is made perfect in weakness. II Corinthians 12:9 NIV

We hear a lot today about efficiency, our homes, cars, appliances, and light bulbs anything that can run and work on less energy is important, but what about sufficient grace? The Bible states that it is more than enough. When you need grace its source is limitless causing all grace to abound in you. This is awesome! The great thing about grace is that it takes less of our energy to work and yet it causes you and me to be more efficient because the all- sufficient one backs it. In your weakness you are made strong. The more you rely on God's cup of grace, the less effort it takes for you to be powerful!

Ask yourself, am I using too much energy trying to serve God instead of allowing God's grace to serve as my strength?

As you read and meditate on this message of grace I pray that your cup will over flow with Christ's all-sufficient grace!

"The all-sufficient grace of Christ is immeasurable!"

∽

Today's Prayer: Father God Thank you for your all-sufficient grace that sustains me today. Amen

Insights

Day 6

THE CUP OF FORGIVENESS

For if you forgive men when they sin against you, your heavenly Father will also forgive you. But if you do not forgive men their sins, your Father will not forgive your sins.
Matthew 6:14 NIV

Jesus spoke these words right after teaching his disciples how to pray. In this prayer he says, "forgive us our debts, as we also forgiven our debtors." It seems the only condition of forgiveness is to do it. You expect God to forgive you of your sins but he expects the same from you towards others. Forgiveness then becomes an act of your will and should become a lifestyle. How can you drink the cup of forgiveness unless you pour out forgiveness? When you live this way you show that the love of God is in you.

Ask yourself, how well do I forgive and do I need forgiveness as much as I need to forgive more?

As you read and meditate on Matt. 6:14 I pray that you freely receive the cup of forgiveness that God's word promises as you freely offer it to others today!

"The price of forgiveness has been paid for, Offer yours freely!"

⌒

Today's Prayer: Father I make a decision to forgive others in my heart today so I can receive your forgiveness freely through communion. Amen

INSIGHTS

Day 7

THE CUP OF CLEANSING

Having therefore these promises, dearly beloved, let us cleanse ourselves from all filthiness of the flesh and spirit, perfecting holiness in the fear of God. II Corinthians 7:1 KJV

Name your favorite laundry detergent and they each claim brighter colors and whiter clothes. The power to cleanse is what Jesus blood promises. There are many hymns of the Church that proclaim the cleansing power and healing of the blood of Christ. The question, "What can wash away my sins?" The answer, "Nothing but the blood of Jesus." This sounds like a modern day cheer going back and forth across a large stadium at a ball game. This is the cheer of heaven and earth, the blood that Jesus shed will never lose its power. "Power, Power, wonder working power in the blood of the lamb." And one of my favorites "O the blood of Jesus, O the blood of Jesus, O the blood of Jesus, it washes white as snow!" Whatever cleansing you need you can come to him for it according to I John 1:9, "He is faithful and just to cleanse us of all unrighteousness."

Ask yourself, have I been to Jesus for the cleansing flood, am I washed in the blood of the lamb today?

As you read and meditate on II Corinthians chapter seven, I pray you receive a cleansing flood of God's love today!

"The cleansing flood of Jesus blood never stops!"

⟲

*Today's Prayer: Father as I receive communion today I thank
you for your cleansing in my heart. Amen*

Insights

Day 8

The Cup of Remembrance

This cup is the new covenant in my blood; do this, whenever you drink it, in remembrance of me. I Corinthians 11:25 NIV

Have you ever forgotten something and wondered what it was that you were thinking about? Perhaps it was just a simple cup of coffee left behind, when you remember it, the coffee is cold. Maybe it's the self-induced preoccupation with agendas and attempts to supersede yesterday's record of accomplishment that distracts us. Even an event of great significance, one in which we can only thank God for His presence of grace, can so easily slip our minds. This has and can happen to anyone, especially when a cloud of emotion is ruling the thought process on any given day.

Christ understood this well and pled with his young pioneering ambassadors, even as they experienced his sustaining presence, the moment would come when they would have to stop and remember the purpose for which be came. It didn't take long for these young ambassadors to come face to face with the reality of those very words. Soon they would remember the one they saw time after time demonstrate the very things that they would need to practice and focus on. Like remembering when the water was turned to wine, or when the woman was healed instantly after twelve years of suffering or the feeding of five thousand. Even in the last hours, when their leader restored the ear of the man who came to take him away to his death.

Today as you partake of the Passover, take a moment to reflect on things forgotten.

Consider the presence of his grace within past times of trouble, or when God made a way when there was no other way.

Raul Orriols

"Remember what God has done for you!"

Today's Prayer: Father I receive this meal of communion as I remember what was done that day for me on the cross. Amen

INSIGHTS

Day 9

THE CUP OF MARRIAGE

For this reason a man will leave his father and mother and be
united to his wife, and they will become one flesh.
Genesis 2:24 NIV

My parents recently celebrated their 60th wedding anniversary, what an amazing testimony in our day and age. But listen to this, I celebrated my 21st, my oldest brother 40th, and everyone in between us reached a mark in marriage of twenty, thirty and now forty. I am the youngest of five and though my sibling's children have not reached any such milestones yet I believe they will. Unfortunately we know first hand the pain and conflicts of divorce. I know why God hates divorce. But I am so thankful we serve a God that can turn our mess into a message of love and hope for anyone who has gone through this loneliness and rejection. My wife and I experienced first hand love beyond rejection and it has been our anchor. Love never fails it believes all things, hopes all things, endures all things and rejoices in the truth. That is a powerful portion of II Corinthians 13, the love chapter, if read everyday it would change so much of our attitudes toward one another. God is love and he instituted the family by putting his seal of blessing on marriage when we keep our eyes on Christ. Husbands are told to love their wives as Christ loved the Church. This is a profound statement.

Ask yourself, can I live a life that love's the way Christ loves the Church?

As you read and meditate on these passages I pray you experience Christ love that is like marriage in your life today!

"Longevity is not the only measure of a good Marriage but it helps"

Today's Prayer: Thank you Father that marriage is a covenant relationship between a man and woman and that vows are sacred like the bread and wine of the New Covenant. Amen

INSIGHTS

Day 10

THE CUP OF WORSHIP

Yet a time is coming and has now come when the true worshipers will worship the Father in spirit and truth, for they are the kind of worshipers the Father seeks, God is Spirit and his worshipers must worship in spirit and in truth.
John 4:23,24 NIV

There is a lot of focus on worship these days and yet most of it is centered around the style of music, or the package one form of worship is delivered in. Clashing cultures and generation gaps have prompted many heated debates surrounding this subject. But what is true worship? As much as I like certain styles of music, the question becomes, is it a necessity of worship or just a tool for worship? Does using music make it spirit and truth or does it just add flavor to the atmosphere of our songs? It is really a matter of the heart, as the one song says, "I'm coming back to the heart of worship where it is all about you," and this should be the true spirit of our hearts. Everything we do in life is a form of worship to God when your life is focused on him, your job, your home, your recreation, your finances and your Church, can all be about worship. Praise and worship music is just one expression of many ways we can worship in spirit and in truth. What kind of worshiper are you?

Ask yourself, is my worship for me or is it all about Christ?

As you read and meditate on this passage I pray that you will discover the true cup of worship for yourself today!

"You and I were made to Worship!"

Today's Prayer: Father help me recognize my whole life is made to worship you. Amen

INSIGHTS

The Second Quarter

PROTECT THE PLACE OF WORSHIP

Now that you have completed the first quarter of your challenge the next assignment is to protect the place of worship. After Noah built an altar and God established His covenant with him he proceeded to plant a vineyard in Genesis 9:20. It is important for you to proceed and begin to plant the seeds of intimacy with God in your life. Prayer, study God's word, worship in song, meditation and communion are vital to this as well as finding a place to plant yourself in relationships with other believers. The Apostles gathered daily to encourage one another and fellow believers. This is how God helps tend to your needs through fellowship with others.

In John 15 Jesus describes our relationship with him and the Father that He is the true vine and the Father is the gardener. We are the branches of the vine and apart from him we cannot do anything according to verse 5. By faith you allow the Holy Spirit to work in you everyday through the process of communion with God. This will please him and he will fill your cup with fresh new wine everyday. (Hebrews 11:6)

If your heart is the centerpiece of your body the temple, shouldn't you do every thing you can to protect it? Proverbs tells us to guard our hearts with all diligence for out of it flows the issues of life. What you hear and what you see effects what you think and will effect what your heart receives. God's word is protection from infection!

In the cup of Nehemiah you will discover the leadership of a cupbearer to take a stand to protect the place of worship. Defense is an important part of a team sport. In football and basketball you may have heard the phrase "protect the ball." It is the same in the spirit realm if worship is the ball then you must "protect it." How do you do that? Quite simply don't let go of what God has freely given you. Meditate on God's word and allow it to begin to penetrate your areas of weakness. The Holy Spirit is your helper or counselor so ask for his assistance in your resistance. So when challenged to defend your worship you can do it through the strength of his Spirit and not in your own strength. Do not allow others to influence your thinking in the midst of this challenge if it is contrary to the covenant. Spit it out like vinegar. Get a drink from the cup of living water, God's word and drink in His Spirit new and fresh. Continue on steadfast; immovable in this journey of a living experience through daily communion with God.

"So I sent messengers to them with this reply: "I am carrying on a great project and cannot go down. Why should the work stop while I leave it and go down to you?" Nehemiah 6:3 NIV

"Defending your Worship will protect your Purpose!"

Prayer: Father God, help me to protect my place of worship by what I allow to come into the eye gate and ear gate of my temple. Amen

Day 11

THE CUP OF NEHEMIAH

So the wall was completed on the twenty-fifth of Elul, in fifty-two days. When all our enemies heard about this, all the surrounding nations were afraid and lost confidence, because they realized that this work had been done with the help of our God. Nehemiah 6:15,16 NIV

Nehemiah was cupbearer to the King in his day. He was one of the most important men to protect the King from drinking anything poison. When Nehemiah heard about the distress that Jerusalem was in he sat down and wept, mourned, fasted and prayed before God. After some four months of this he went before the King and he recognized something was wrong with Nehemiah since he had never been sad in his presence before. After explaining to the King what was wrong the Kings reply was "what is it you want?" The door of opportunity swung wide open but before Nehemiah responded he again prayed. Then he began one of the most remarkable rebuilding projects ever. After surveying the work he had a vision that would require a community of committed believers to accomplish. And so with great opportunity came great opposition but they never stopped building until the work was complete. Nehemiah's vision help to rebuild the walls of Jerusalem in just 52 days, and gave them a fortified city against their enemies. It was all about protecting the place of worship for the people of God. Rebuilding this wall was rebuilding relationships that had been torn down. The best way to protect your place of worship is to connect to other believers in the local church and break bread together.

"Fellowship helps to fortify our place of worship!"

~

Today's Prayer: Father, help me find fellowship with another believer that can help me grow in my walk with you. Amen

INSIGHTS

Day 12

THE CUP OF GETHSEMANE

He went away again the second time, and prayed, saying, O my Father, if this cup may not pass away from me, except I drink it, thy will be done. Matthew 26:42 NIV

After the old rugged cross and the empty tomb, the garden of Gethsemane is arguably the third most significant moment in the life of Jesus. His literal death, burial and resurrection were things only the unblemished Lamb of God could do. But his example in Gethsemane is something every Believer should follow. Gethsemane literally means: "Wine or oil press". A grape or an olive must go through a "press" in order to become useful as wine or oil. In similar fashion, you and I must experience the breaking of the outer man (flesh), in order for the beauty of the inner man (spirit) to come forth. Jesus was not looking forward to bloody torture and a slow death on the Roman cross. Yet in the end, He chose his Father's will instead of his own survival. This is the single most powerful example a Believer can follow. Deny your "self" (meaning your own will, desires, ambitions, ideas, opinions), take up your cross, and follow Him.

In Gethsemane, the Father extended a Cup and held it in front of Jesus. It was the inevitability of the Father's Will. For three solid hours, no matter what Jesus said... no matter how much he pleaded... the Cup remained. The Father's silence spoke loudly. Jesus understood something we all must learn: The only way this Cup will pass, is if you drink it. The dull ache of disobedience is hard to live with.

The holy process of obeying God's will whenever it conflicts with our own will grows more familiar as we mature in Christ. Here's how it works: 1) It always requires death to self. 2) He will place that Cup in front of you and graciously invite you to drink it. If you refuse, you can ignore it for a while, but soon you will find Him placing it squarely in front of your face again. This cycle will repeat itself until you finally get tired of wrestling with God, surrender your will, and choose to drink the Cup He has already chosen for you. O the release! O the sense of peace and oneness with Him! You can almost hear an audible voice as He says: "Well done my good and faithful servant. Enter into the Joy of thy Lord." –Bruce Delay

"The only way the Cup will pass, is if you drink it."

Insights

Day 13

THE CUP OF OFFENSE

Aware that his disciples were grumbling about this, Jesus said to them, "Does this offend you?" John 6:61 NIV

Why is the grass always greener on the other side? It could be we have put up a barrier called "offense". But there is a way to get to the other side. Jesus made a way, the gateway of forgiveness. The grass truly is greener on that side and there are no boundaries in this field. God has deposited this ability to love and forgive into each one of us through the blood of Jesus. Think about these statements, hurt hinders but love heals, pain paralyzes but peace says rise and walk, anger burns bridges while joy celebrates getting to the other side. Any sin is unsettling but forgiveness can settle all. Offense may come but what you do with it will determine whether you enjoy peaceful pastures or a sun scorched land. I have discovered that self is at the root of our offense. God wants to show you something about yourself not the one who offends. If you have been offended you can be mended. Open the gate of forgiveness and enjoy God's way!

Ask yourself, do I offend or am I offended, either way what is God showing me about myself?

As you read and meditate of John 6 I pray that the gate of forgiveness will swing wide open for you today to enjoy God's way!

"The greatest barrier to life is offense!"

Today's Prayer: Father, break down any barriers in my heart that would stop the flow of your forgiveness to me or through me. Amen

Insights

Day 14

THE CUP OF FELLOWSHIP

But if we walk in the light, as he is in the light, we have
fellowship one with another, and the blood of Jesus, his Son,
purifies us from all sin. 1 John 1:7 NIV

Walking in the light of fellowship requires communion with God and other true believers. The early Church lived out this truth in their daily lives breaking bread together from house to house. How awesome is fellowship with our Father, family, friends and other followers of Christ. There are no sweeter times than those you share with the ones you love. Fellowship helps purify your walk. The depth of your fellowship with one another may coincide with the depth of your fellowship with Christ.

Ask yourself, how deep is my fellowship with other believers?

As you read and meditate on 1 John 1 I pray you will take the cup of fellowship and cultivate it as a lifestyle starting today!

"Fellowship is sweet at the Lord's table when we eat!"

~

Today's Prayer: Pray for deeper fellowship with God and others today. Fellowship is to be a lifestyle. Amen

INSIGHTS

Day 15

THE CUP OF UNITY

May they be brought to complete unity to let the world know that you sent me and have loved them even as you have loved me. John 17:23 NIV

This is the prayer Jesus prayed for you and me! Unity as he was one with the Father, he wanted you and me to be one with one another. He could have made it a commandment and yet this would have only caused more division. Unity has to do with your will, though it is his will he made it your choice to walk in unity. Remember to love one another is the commandment. So why can't we agree? Diversity within one body is what Paul taught. To recognize each person's gifts and calling as equally important to the whole body. It takes love, respect, honor and most of all humility. These are attributes that should characterize a true believer. The question then becomes are you one with him in true communion and fellowship?

Think about the loaf of bread as the body of Christ, the church, and the cup of his blood that flows through each of us making you and I members of the same family.

Ask yourself, does my diversity promote unity with other believer's in Christ?

As you read and meditate on John chapter 17, I pray that you will discover this true Cup of Unity in your fellowship with other believers today!

"Breaking the bread of unity breaks division!"

Today's Prayer: Father I pray for unity in my life and in the body of Christ today as I break the bread and drink the cup.
Amen

INSIGHTS

Day 16

THE CUP OF BROTHERS

A friend loves at all times, and a brother is born for adversity.
Proverbs 17:17 NIV

Years ago I often wondered what this verse meant when it said, "a brother is born for adversity". I thought it meant brothers were always going to fight since I had three older brothers and we fought. Naturally my two brothers closest to me picked on me to watch me burn and then blow. It took me a long time to figure out it was there entertainment and if I didn't get mad it would spoiled their fun. It was too late though, they grew up and moved on.

Not until later in life seeing my oldest brother Tim go through adversity did I begin to understand. It's about your brother. Who do you call your brother and whom can you call on? Jesus said, "for whoever does the will of my father in heaven is my brother and sister and mother." God created the family long before the church so the church could have a model, family. Family goes beyond blood relationships and is important in times of trouble. The church can be our family, when you are in relationship, to help in time of need. You will have days of crisis and you will need a brother to lean on.

Ask yourself, do I have a brother or Sister I can call in my time of need?

As you meditate on this passage remember this promise, "...but there is a friend who sticks closer than a brother." Proverbs 18:24*NIV*

"To get the best of both befriend a brother!"

Today's Prayer: Thank God today for brothers and sisters in Christ. Ask God to give you those who will be true to you.
Amen

INSIGHTS

Day 17

THE CUP OF ONE

There is one body and one Spirit-just as you were called to one hope when you were called-one Lord, one faith, one baptism; one God and Father of all, who is over all and through all and in all. Ephesians 4:4-6 NIV

There is a popular song with the lyrics "one is the loneliest number that you'll ever know." I have also heard the saying "it is lonely at the top." In competitive sports it is all about being number one. A legendary NASCAR driver had a passion for being number one. His car however had the infamous number three on it. This makes me think of the mystery of the triune God. The doxology says, "God in three persons, blessed trinity." Your passion should be focused on the mystery, majesty and masterpiece of the one true God; that works in unison Father, Son and Holy Spirit. The word of God tells you that the cords of three are not easily broken. Jesus prayed that we would be as one. In team sports the goal is to be number one and yet everyone has a part to play and must contribute according to their purpose. Even in NASCAR the unsung heroes are often those in the pit crew. The faster and more efficient they perform the better.

Ask yourself, what is the common denominator in my life? Am I trying to live alone as one?

As you read and meditate on Ephesians chapter four remember the one who is in your pit crew today!

"One thing may not define my life, but one thing has changed my life, so my life can be defined."

⸜⸝

Today's Prayer: Father I thank you for the one true body of Christ you died for, rose for and you are coming for! Amen

INSIGHTS

Day 18

The Cup of Service

Serve wholeheartedly, as if you were serving the Lord, not men, because you know that the Lord will reward everyone for whatever good he does, whether he is slave or free.
Ephesians 6:7,8 NIV

If you act as you desire in the service of others, are you truly serving them? Is not service the act of filling the need of others, with no secondary motive of our own? We can only know what others really need by communicating with them. Service is, knowing the thing that is causing their distress, and doing what you can to aid them in overcoming that "thing". You and I tend to want to over help, but this can cause more harm than you might know. Being of service is really a simple act. It is as uncomplicated as merely being available. Service is a gift, not a loan. You should strive to give what is needed, not what you "think" is needed. The good intentions you may believe are the answer, often have no effect on the need. Love and listen... you will be told how to serve!

Bob Hill (The Coffee Guy)

"We best serve God by serving others!"

Today's Prayer: Father as I receive your body and blood and am asking for a heart to serve others Amen

INSIGHTS

Day 19

THE CUP OF PURE JOY

Consider it pure joy, my brothers, whenever you face trails of many kinds, James 1:2 NIV

This scripture is all about building character in believers but isn't it odd to use trials as a means for joy? No pain no gain. Another translation reads "count it all joy". You mean everything! If everything is pointing to God in the end isn't that the point.

What makes the joy pure is the motive set forth within it. That is how Jesus lived it out in Hebrews 12:2 NIV it says, "…for the joy set before him he endured the cross, scorning its shame." Seeing a future hope helps us realize joy while enduring pain and suffering. There is light at the end of the tunnel.

Ask yourself, have my motives been pure in my pain that I can experience Joy even in suffering?

God's promise is that all things work together for the good of those who love Him according to Romans 8:28. As you read and meditate on James 1 I pray that you encounter Pure Joy today in Christ!

"Pure Joy comes in the first light of day!"

Today's Prayer: Father teach me to rejoice in my trails so I can learn the meaning of pure joy. Amen

INSIGHTS

Day 20

THE CUP OF BROKENNESS

The sacrifices of God are a broken spirit; a broken and contrite heart, O God, you will not despise. Psalms 51:17 NIV

Have you ever had one of those days when everything seems broken? Nothing seems to be able to be mended. Your best effort to say a kind word does not come across kind. Everything is broken, the car, the bank account, relationships it's all broken. Is this God's will? No, but it could be your pathway of discovering true brokenness. You see to be broken is not a matter of what is going on outside but what position our hearts are in inside. God wants you to be broken of pride, arrogance, envy, or any heart issue that does not show the life and love of God. When you become broken in your spirit the way God wants you, he will touch your senses about everything. You will understand what God meant when he said to love your neighbor as yourself. If you love your life you cannot fully love others, if you love yourself you really can! Life isn't about the stuff that you have but it's about the stuff inside you. It is what God puts in you that you have to learn to love and not what your career has afforded you. When you begin to feel the pressing of God's love on your life welcome it with an open heart. You will become broken but not broke!

Ask yourself, do I love my life more than I love myself?

As you read and meditate on Psalms 51 I pray that you discover brokenness through the love of God today!

45

"Broken does not mean broke!"

⁓

Today's Prayer: Father God, keep me broken to the things of this world so I can be whole in you. Amen

INSIGHTS

The Third Quarter

Keep Pursuing God

David was considered by God to be "a man after his own heart." What are you chasing in your own life? It's the third quarter of the challenge and what you are receiving daily will sustain you. That is exactly how David continued after many mistakes was confessing his sin and getting back into communion with God. Even though he himself was a King he just would not stop pursuing God. Now is not the time to give up but to reach up and take hold of the cross that is before you. The way of the cross is uncomfortable at times but it is the only way to the promise of the covenant. Christ found joy through obedience even though it meant death on the cross. Hebrews 11:7 NIV "By faith Noah, when warned about things not yet seen, in holy fear built an ark to save his family. By his faith he condemned the world and became heir of the righteousness that comes by faith."

Noah's pursuit of God saved his family. God's laws are fixed and they are as sure as gravity, they will continue to pull us back to him. Isn't that an awesome thought that God's Spirit will continue to draw you to him as you continue to pursue him! God does not want you to fail but to prevail. Continue the good fight of faith so in enduring your own cross you can win in this amazing challenge called the cup (life)!

"After removing Saul, he made David their king. He testified concerning him: 'I have found David son of Jesse a man

after my own heart; he will do everything I want him to do."
Acts 13:22 NIV

"God is pursuing us as much as we are pursuing him!"

~

Prayer: Father God, as I pursue you my prayer is you catch me, hold me, and never let me go! Amen

Day 21

THE CONTAMINATED CUP

Again Jesus called the crowd to him and said, "Listen to me, everyone, and understand this. Nothing outside a man can make him 'unclean' by going into him. Rather, it is what comes out of a man that makes him 'unclean'." Mark 7:14,15 NIV

Tainted Love was a popular song in the 80s. It reminds me of myself when I look at my love for God. Many times I have become contaminated or tainted by the things of this world. Contamination refers to coming in contact to make something impure, unclean or unfit. This is exactly what happens when your walk with God is contaminated by your sinful nature. What others see from the outside of the cup may look pure, but it is what is inside the cup that makes it impure. Wrong motives, jealousy, strife, envy and other attributes of the flesh are at war in you. When your heart is tainted with lust and corrupt it will be seen sooner or later. What you put in your cup, (heart) will eventually come out. Conforming on the outside to what looks right does not make one pure. Though you go to church, volunteer, do lots of good deeds this will not justify or make right your heart. Only the blood of Jesus can do that.

Ask yourself, has my cup been contaminated by what I put in it?

As you read and meditate on Mark 7 I pray God will wash you deep within with the precious blood of Christ today!

"What you put in your cup will eventually come out!"

Today's Prayer: Father help me keep the heart of my temple pure before you as I receive the bread of life and the cup of forgiveness through communion today. Amen

INSIGHTS

Day 22

THE CUP OF DEATH

When the perishable has been clothed with the imperishable, and the mortal with immortality, then the saying that is written will come true: "Death has been swallowed up in victory." Where O Death, is your victory? Where, O Death, is your sting? I Corinthians 15:54,55 NIV

Death is a means to life. Everyday you live you will be faced with death in some form. Choosing to die to yourself is the greatest challenge you have to overcome as you live. Living is a choice just as dying becomes a choice as well. I cannot live unless I die, the more I die the more I live.

Physical death will come as your days are numbered, but spiritual life and death have two choices. God gives you the choice and says, Choose life. Paul said, "to live is Christ and to die is gain."

Ask your self, am I living to die or dying to live?

As you read and meditate on I Corinthians chapter fifteen, I pray you choose life today, so in dying you can live!

"Death is sure so choose life!"

Today's Prayer: Father God I thank you for giving me life through the body and blood of Jesus Christ my Lord and Savior. I thank you for the empty tomb because he lives I can live life more fully. Amen

INSIGHTS

Day 23

THE CUP OF COMPASSION

And Jesus, moved with compassion, put forth his hand, and touched him, and saith unto him, I will; be thou clean.
Mark 1:41 KJV

This is only one example of many in the scripture where Jesus was moved with compassion seeing a need and meeting it. His compassion was not limited to individuals but upon seeing the multitude he was moved with compassion. He fed 5,000, raised the dead, healed the sick and delivered those possessed by demons. It all started with an inward emotion we call compassion.

As it has been said necessity is the mother of invention, could compassion be the father of miracles? In James 1:22 NIV it says "Do not merely listen to the word, and so deceive yourselves, but do what it says." The heart of the matter is how do you view the needs of others?

Ask yourself, what compels you or moves you to action?

As you read and meditate on the compassion of Christ may this cup of compassion fill you with his passion for others today!

"Compassion is to be encompassed with Christ's Passion!"

Today's Prayer: Father open my heart to receive compassion to see others needs and respond. Amen

INSIGHTS

Day 24

The Cup of Sacrifice

Such a high priest meets our need-one who is holy, blameless, pure, set apart from sinners, exalted above the heavens. Unlike the other high priests, he does not need to offer sacrifices day after day, first for his sins and then for the sins of the people. He sacrificed for their sins once for all when he offered himself.
Hebrews 7:26,27 NIV

The ultimate sacrifice is what Jesus gave. He himself said "there is no greater love than this, than to lay down your life for your brother." Thankfully the word sacrifice does not have to be a negative one. It is a word however of faith, patience and obedience. Obedience to do what God commands, patience to allow him to work through us and faith to believe that what he said he will do. This is the progression to be obedient in sacrifice, patient to wait for God's promise and faith to receive it. Sacrifice could be the first and last step to breakthrough!

Remember as you take the cup that Christ's sacrifice is enough to meet your need today, however great it is!

As you read and meditate on Hebrews seven, I pray you receive the blessing of our high priest today!

"Sacrifice could be the first and last step to breakthrough!"

Today's Prayer: Ask God to show you how to live out sacrifice through faith, patience and obedience. Amem

INSIGHTS

Day 25

THE CUP OF TRUTH

Then you will know the truth, and the truth will set you free.
John 8:32 NIV

The battle between believing and knowing stand in opposite corners of one another. One says I believe in Jesus, the other saying I know Jesus. The scripture says even the demons believe and tremble. That's a scary thought! I can believe and not know. Jesus said, "if you hold to my teachings, you are really my disciples." Knowledge of the truth then comes through the gateway of discipline. God's truth can set you free in an instant, but to stay free you need discipline to continue pursuing truth. Pursue Christ with your life and you will find truth. Remember truth is not what, but who, "Jesus Christ is the same yesterday and today and forever." according to Hebrews 13:8 NIV.

Ask yourself, am I held captive in areas of my life because I don't have the knowledge of truth?

As you read and meditate on this passage I pray you will receive His cup of truth and become free today!

"Truth is not a what but a who!"
Bruce Delay

Today's Prayer: Thank you Father that Jesus is the truth and His body and blood are the tangible evidence of that in my life today. Amen

INSIGHTS

Day 26

THE CUP THAT TRANSFORMS

*Do not conform any longer to the pattern of this world, but be
transformed by the renewing of your mind.*
Romans 12:2a NIV

I remember my daughter when she was very young and
she began to learn about patterns. Sequences of numbers,
colors or designs that would repeat themselves. She got so
excited when she got it and would point and say "that's a
pattern." She is eight now and still points them out. There is
a pattern throughout God's word you need to discover for
yourself. This pattern is what transforms you. Many times
you are only conformed to change by outward influences.
The world around you wants you to conform to their ways,
how they talk and act. On the other hand to allow one's self
to be transformed takes a changing of mind which is the
same as repentance, to change and go another way. Discovering the truth in God's word is what will transform you
from the inside out. The pattern of the world is full of lies
that will cause you to conform to what ever is popular. The
pattern of God's word is full of grace and truth and His love
to redeem you from this world.

Ask yourself, am I conforming too much to the world
around me?

As you read and meditate on Romans chapter 12, I pray
you will have a transforming experience in your life today!

"Lies Conform but Truth Transforms"

Today's Prayer: Father God I thank you for transforming my life through daily communion with you. Renew my mind as I receive it today. Amen

INSIGHTS

Day 27

THE CUP OF NERDS

I keep asking that the God of our Lord Jesus Christ, the glorious Father, may give you the Spirit of wisdom and revelation, so that you may know him better. Ephesians 1:17 NIV

Have you ever had one of those moments when during a sermon something happens inside. I call it "NERDS," newly encountered revelations during sermons. Come on you know what I'm talking about, that moment when your brain catches up with your spirit and for the next ten minutes your chasing a thought you had never had before. In the meantime the minister has gone on for another ten minutes about his own NERDS, but you didn't even get them, because you are still chewing on that one! One is as good as a handful if you take the time to enjoy it. Maybe it was all you needed for that day. The rest was for everyone else who likes NERDS!

Ask yourself, have I had any newly encountered revelations during sermons lately?

As you read and meditate on Ephesians 1:15-22 I pray you will receive a full cup of NERDS today!

"NERDS-newly encountered revelations during sermons"

Today's Prayer: Father, thank you for revealing your son Jesus Christ to me today through the bread and wine. I receive the revelation of your Holy Spirit. Amen

INSIGHTS

Day 28

The Cup of Relevance

Jesus Christ is the same yesterday and today and forever.
Hebrews 13:8 NIV

I hear this buzz word a lot these days about being relevant. People want something relevant for their lives or just to be relevant in ministry. Webster's dictionary defines relevant as bearing upon or related to the matter in hand; pertinent; to the point. The last one I really think sums up my thought on relevance. Truth is to the point, my point exactly. Truth never changes therefore it is always relevant. It does not age or become outdated, it's dependable, reliable, and believable and has value when spoken. Truth always prevails so it will always be relevant. If you want to be relevant find truth and you will stand out in darkness. Truth is pointing the way in every generation.

Ask yourself, what impact is truth having in my life to make my life relevant?

As you read and meditate on this passage I pray His cup of relevance will point the way to more truth today!

"Today you are relevant because he is truth"

⤳

Today's Prayer: Pray that your words will be full of truth and relevance today. Amen

INSIGHTS

Day 29

THE CUP OF MERCY

For the Lord your God is a merciful God; he will not abandon or destroy you or forget the covenant with your forefathers, which he confirmed to them by oath. Deuteronomy 4:31 NIV

Mercy in laymen's terms is withholding from you what you deserve, while grace is giving you what you do not deserve. You see the term mercy and merciful used throughout the Old Testament. God was constantly withholding or delaying judgment on people who deserved judgment. Only because God is compassionate he would give people opportunity to repent so they could avoid judgment. Today you and I deserved to be judged as much as anyone, but the cross of calvery made the difference! The cross unveiled a side of God that had not yet been understood, grace, undeserved or unmerited favor. The only judgment you receive is by choice, choosing not to believe in the blood sacrifice of Jesus Christ. There is no mercy for someone who rejects Christ nor will there be any grace. As believer's you are called to show mercy, in other words do not pass judgment quickly on anyone. "He has showed you, O man, what is good. And what does the Lord require of you? To act justly and to love mercy and to walk humbly with your God." Micah 6:8 NIV. This is the best of judges one can find.

Ask yourself, am I merciful to those around me?

As you read and meditate on this passage I pray God teach you from the cup of mercy today!

"Show mercy often and you will receive mercy often"

⌒

Today's Prayer: Ask God to help you love mercy and show it more often. Amen

INSIGHTS

Day 30

THE CUP OF DREAMS

For you created my inmost being; you knit me together in my mother's womb. I praise you because I am fearfully and wonderfully made; your works are wonderful, I know them full well. Psalms 139:13,14 NIV

Here we are at the table again, breaking bread and drinking from the cup; thinking of all that Christ is to our life, our family and friends. As I sipped on my cup of joe at first light I began to see images in my head of future possibilities. I saw myself doing some amazing things that were totally beyond my ability to comprehend them. It appeared as a huge cup of dreams that the Lord was pouring out just for me.

You and I are given an incredible imagination that our Heavenly Father desired for us to use so that we could see things in the future and get excited about them. He has poured out a cup of dreams for everyone that would dare to drink it. Unfortunately for many this cup of dreams goes cold. It remains untouched as life circumstances and the busyness of the daily grind distract us. By the time we have realized what has happened and go back to the cup, it's too cold to enjoy.

The Good News this morning is that your cup of dreams can be warmed up again. The warmth of God's Spirit is like a divine microwave, which can get you drinking from that cup again, seeing yourself doing incredible things and enjoying every minute of it!

– Joe Jones

"Dreams require you to get outside yourself so that you can see within yourself"
Cup of Joe

⌣

Today's Prayer: Ask God to give you a dream if you do not have one. Your dream is tied directly to your purpose when it's focused on God's purposes. Amen

INSIGHTS

The Fourth Quarter

PASSION FOR HIS PRESENCE

Have you ever thought what it would be like to live in the presence of a King? "One night with the King" was a great movie about Esther and how God used her to save her people. This is the most important part of the challenge, the last ten days, the last quarter. How do you think it will effect your life or has it already? How you finish is more important in life than how you started.

A great story was told to me recently about a man named Obed-Edom the Gettite. Okay it's true it is in the Bible, but I had just never had light shed on it like this. Obed-Edom was an ordinary man that had been converted and circumcised to become a Jew. He was not born into it but adopted. But something amazing happened one day. The Ark of the Covenant was being transported to Jerusalem when someone touched the ark and died. David was so afraid he asked how could he bring the ark to his house? He told Obed-Edom to take it to his house, where it remained for three months. Can you imagine the ark of God's covenant where his presence dwelt being in your house? Long story short Obed-Edom's house was blessed and after David got it and brought it back, Obed-Edom could never leave the presence of God again. He ended up moving into the temple, from janitor to the choir to musician! His life was transformed forever by the presence of God! I pray that you will have a living experience like Obed-Edom and never want to leave the presence of God again as you continually commune with him! We must become passionate about God's pres-

69

ence! If the seeds of intimacy are to remain and produce in our lives they must be saturated in the presence of God.
Jon Paul Tucker

"The ark of God remained with the family of Obed-Edom in his house for three months, and the Lord blessed his household and everything he had." 1 Chronicles 13:14 NIV

"The time and place is now for God's Presence!

Prayer: Father, Fill my cup to overflowing with your presence as I seek you. Amen

INSIGHTS

Day 31

THE CUP OF REDEMPTION

In him we have redemption through his blood, the forgiveness
of sins, in accordance with the riches of God's grace.
Ephesians 1:7 NIV

Are you ready for this! The "R" factor, this is "R" cup!
These are five reasons to receive this cup.

♦ Redemption – we are redeemed by his blood!
(Col. 1:14)

♦ Restoration – we are restored to relationship with
Christ! (Jn. 11:25)

♦ Revelation – he reveals himself to us! (Jn.
16:29,30)

♦ Relevance –we are released in truth that transforms generations! (Jn. 8:32)

♦ Reward –we receive Righteousness, peace and joy
in the Holy Ghost! (Rom. 14:17)

Five more benefits of Redemption.

♦ We receive Rest from works because of grace!
(Eph. 2:8,9)

- ◆ We Reap fruit in our lives! (Jn. 15:5)
- ◆ We Rejoice always! (Phil. 4:4)
- ◆ We receive Riches in Heaven! (Matt. 6:20,21)
- ◆ We are bought with a price, paid for by Christ! Let the Redeemed of the Lord say so. (I Cor. 6:20, Ps. 107:2)

Ask yourself, have I been receiving all the benefits God has in his plan of Redemption for me?

As you read and meditate on this message of Redemption I pray that the cup of redemption redeem everything in you today!

"The cup of Redemption is complete so drink it in!"

Today's Prayer: Before you pray today spend a little extra time reading the above scriptures. Then thank God for His complete plan of Redemption as you receive communion today. Amen

INSIGHTS

Day 32

THE CUP OF MY FATHER

For ye have not received the spirit of bondage again to fear; but ye have received the Spirit of adoption, whereby we cry, Abba, Father. Romans 8:15 KJV

I can only imagine what it would be like to have been an orphan. I was blessed with a loving earthly Father. Even though I was a spiritual orphan as we all are before excepting Christ. To be Fatherless is the most heart wrenching experience for any child. The term Abba that is used in scripture means, Daddy, this comes from the Jewish culture and is what the children would call their Fathers. The term Father seems for some to be an authoritative figurehead, and is hard to see as loving. The term Daddy on the other hand is seen as tender, loving, caring compassionate and all knowing one that loves me no matter what. When you first come to God you come in fear knowing He knows your sin but as you stand before Him, fear is melted away by love and you are suddenly embraced and encompassed by Abba, Father. Daddy God you cry inside as the joy of a child fills your heart you want to do nothing but run to him every time you fall, every time you hurt, every time you succeed, every time!

Ask yourself, do I run to God every time, or am I running from him?

As you read and meditate on Romans 8, I pray that the Father embrace you with the love of Daddy today!

"My heart cries out for Daddy God!"

Today's Prayer: Thank you Father God for being a Daddy to me and not leaving me Fatherless. Amen

INSIGHTS

Day 33

THE CUP OF LIFE

But whoever drinks the water I give him will never thirst. Indeed, the water I give him will become in him a spring of water welling to eternal life. John 4:14 NIV

What can quench the deep hollow thirst of a man's soul? They don't bottle this drink anywhere and yet many try to fill this void with the emptiness of the cares and sorrows of this world and still the thirst gets stronger. What can satisfy this inward thirst that drives you to this search for more?

The woman at the well needed something more and yet what she was thirsty for revealed a real life issue that only Jesus could help her with. The Cup of Life exposes you to life, as you know it, a bitter life of sin turned sweet only by a drink of His Life. Christ poured out his blood on the cross so that your life could be filled with His life. Without this shedding of blood there is no remission of sin.

Ask yourself, has the Cup of Life been dammed up by the cares of this world?

As you meditate and read from John the 4th chapter I pray that the spring of water begin to flow through you and you are continually filled by the Cup of Life Today!

"Life in him is the only life worth living!"

⌒

Today's Prayer: Celebrate the body and blood of Christ today through communion and thank Him for everlasting life. Amen

INSIGHTS

Day 34

Mom's Cup of Communion

The cup of blessing which we bless, is it not the communion of the blood of Christ? The bread which we break, is it not the communion of the body of Christ? 1 Corinthians 10:16 KJV

Recently my brother Stan asked our mother to write a short commentary on communion. As usual my mom does not stray from the word of God. This is what she wrote after the verse above.

Verse 17-"For we being many are one bread and one body: for we are all partakers of that one bread. Verse 21-"Ye cannot drink the cup of the Lord, and the cup of devils. John 17:11- prayer of Jesus that they may be one, as we are one! Repeated in John 17:21-22 and John 6:53,54.

Matthew 26:26-29 The New Covenant.

Acts 2:42,46 Christian Fellowship.

Luke 22:17,19

Communion binds us together as we partake of His body and blood we become one.

As oft as ye do it: do it unto me – in remembrance of me. Ye is singular!

1 Corinthians 11:25,26

Thank you Mom, you are always true to the word.

I pray as you read and meditate on the scriptures above you experience your own cup of communion today!

"God Bless the cup of Blessing!"

⌒

Today's Prayer: Father God I thank you for mom's everywhere who love and care for their children. Amen

INSIGHTS

Day 35

THE CUP OF LIBERTY

Now the Lord is that Spirit: and where the Spirit of the Lord is, there is liberty. II Corinthians 3:17 KJV

Americans tend to flaunt their freedom given to us by our founding fathers, life, liberty and the pursuit of happiness. That is their right, right? As believer's this liberty should come with great conviction and deep joy. It is a three-fold message. God breathed into you the breath of life, His Spirit, filled you with his love, His Spirit, and called you to walk in the liberty of His Spirit. Life, love and liberty are tied together like three cords in one Spirit. Peace and unity become the core attributes of this. To know true love is to be at peace with God. To experience abundant life you must know the love of God. To grasp the liberty of the Spirit there must be love and unity among us. Liberty comes with a price, responsibility to God. I experienced true unity recently at a women prayer group at a Catholic Church. There were four of us men there, United Methodist, Anglican, Asian, Hispanic, young and old. No race, creed, color or gender could keep these women from loving God and loving others and allow the Spirit of liberty to manifest. It truly was awesome!

Ask yourself, have I taken the responsibility for my liberty in Christ?

As you read and meditate on II Corinthians 3, I pray that the Spirit will set you free so you can walk in His life, love and liberty today!

"Liberty comes with great responsibility."

～

Today's Prayer: Father give me liberty in my spirit today! Amen

INSIGHTS

Day 36

THE CUP OF CONFIRMATION

"For I know the plans I have for you," declares the Lord, "Plans to prosper you and not to harm you, plans to give you hope and a future." Jeremiah 29:11 NIV

In every word this is truth. He does have a plan for all of us that will not harm us but will prosper us as well as give us a future. When faced with adversity we as believers sometimes forget this written confirming word that supersedes all understanding.

I John 4:4 says, "You, dear children, are from God and have overcome them, because greater is he that is in you than he that is in the world!" You know whom he is referring to when he says he that is in the world. You already have the victory. It's a done deal. You have the authority to tread on the serpents and the scorpions, and power over the entire enemy: and nothing by any means shall hurt you. Ephesians 6:12 says, "For we wrestle not against flesh and blood, but against spiritual wickedness in high places. Isn't it awesome that we have God backing us in our corner?

These are just a couple of examples of confirmation that no matter what you are faced with, God is on your side even when it looks like you are going to lose...God is on your side. The battle has already been won and you are on the winning side. It is up to you to exercise your spiritual right as believer's to stand in the gap, pray for the lost and praise the Lord for you have the victory!

–Tony

"No hope, no future, know hope and you will have a future!"

Today's Prayer: Father God I believe you are confirming the word of your covenant through communion in my life today.
Amen

INSIGHTS

Day 37

THE CUP OF PASSION

I want to know Christ and the power of his resurrection and the fellowship of sharing in sufferings, becoming like him in his death, and so, somehow, to attain to the resurrection from the dead. Philippians 3:10 NIV

The movie made by Mel Gibson "The Passion" was one of the greatest films of the crucifixion of Christ. Much like the movie "Saving Private Ryan" those who were there said it was as close to the real thing as you could get. If Christ could sit with us and watch "The Passion" I am convinced He would probably feel the same way about this work. When you reflect on passion you identify with suffering because this is the root meaning of the word. If you desire a passionate lifestyle with Christ it will require suffering. Many believers only want the glory of resurrection and not to identify with the suffering Christ endured to have that opportunity. The fellowship of his suffering is taking up your own cross and following him. Why did eleven men die for the cause of Christ? Do you think that they died for a lie? They saw him, knew him and were convinced he is the truth! No man will knowingly die for a lie. Men are still dying today for this person known as truth. Passion may be painful at times, but without it promise cannot be proclaimed. Endure what you can give him what you can't!

Ask yourself, am I passionate about Christ passion or just his promises?

As you read and meditate on the sufferings of Christ I pray you will live with new appreciation of passion today!

"Passion and Promise are wrapped up in one convincing truth, Christ!"

∽

Today's Prayer: Father give me passion in my heart and life today. Amen

INSIGHTS

Day 38

The Cup of Passover

This is a day you are to commemorate; for the generations to come you shall celebrate it as a festival to the Lord-a lasting ordinance. Exodus 12:14 NIV

God established a lasting ordinance the first night of Passover. He had spoken to Moses and promised deliverance, "I will free you from being slaves to them and redeem you with an outstretched arm and with mighty acts of judgment." Exodus 6:6 NIV That promise and that ordinance became the covenant Jesus sealed with his own blood. Jesus said, "I am the door", and with outstretched arms he shed his innocent blood and marked the passageway so that death would Passover us. Every time you break bread and drink the cup of the Lord you celebrate Passover! The Old Testament was only a foreshadowing of things to come through Christ. You who were once in darkness can now see through the true light that has come.

There are four cups taken in a Passover seder, they are the cup of sanctification, plagues, redemption and praise. God said not only to commemorate but to celebrate! Exodus 12:17. The last cup, the cup of praise, reminds you to rejoice in what God has delivered you from!

I pray that today as you commemorate you also celebrate with a song of praise, thanking God for his mighty hand of deliverance!

"Commemorate, Celebrate, Passover!"

Today's Prayer: God I thank you for the outstretched arms of Christ that saves me today. Amen

Insights

Day 39

THE CUP OF POWER

Now to him who is able to do exceeding abundantly beyond all that we ask of think, according to the power that works within us. Ephesians 3:20 NAS

Do you understand the cup of power that's being offered to you and I who believe? When the King of all glory fills your cup it truly is immeasurable. He has given you His power to do things for His glory. His power is His Spirit and the Bible says in Romans 8:11 that the Spirit of him who raised Jesus from the dead is living in you. This is not some mystical power to be used to lavish yourself with worldly desires but the power to change your life. Apart from this power you have no hope in life. This is the original power drink. The power to forgive. The power to love. The power to do what He has called you to do. What's your cup filled with today? Could it be Loneliness, bitterness, a bad relationship, lack of finances, doubt, confusion, or any other negative thing? A lot of times you can't just empty the cup. I know when you put the coffee cup under the running kitchen faucet whether you've emptied it or not the water flushes out everything in the cup. When you leave it there long enough and it overflows then all the contents become clear and clean. That's what the power of the communion cup can do for you today!

Pray today that the Father gives you the power to live your life and to do the things you have been called to do.

–Stan Tucker

"His power is Resurrection Power!"

Today's Prayer: Father I ask you for the power of your Holy Spirit to demonstrate power in my life today. Amen

INSIGHTS

Day 40

THE CUP OF PROVISION

Solomon's daily provisions were thirty cors of fine flour and sixty cors of meal, ten head of stall-fed cattle, twenty of pasture-fed cattle and a hundred sheep and goats, as well as deer, gazelles, roebucks and choice fowl. I Kings 4:22,23 NIV

Isn't it amazing that Solomon's daily provisions were recorded in the Bible for you to read? Why do you think that it mattered? Maybe God just wanted to show you just how much he cares for your daily needs. Jesus said your Father knows what you need before you ask. Do you really know what you need daily? Does God have a list of your needs in heaven he looks over daily? I am thankful for God's hand of provision in my life. He has fed me and led me. He has provided a way for you through the body and blood of Jesus. Just like he provided a ram for Abraham, manna in the desert, the cross has provided every need you have spirit, soul and body. We lack nothing in him! If you break down the word provision it is pro-vision. Pro means for you and God is always for your vision! Where he guides, he will provide. It may not be in the form you desire at the time, but it will sustain you daily. The Bible says if God is for us who can be against us? Romans 8:31

Ask yourself, am I trusting God in my journey that he has already provided?

As you read and meditate on God's provision I pray that you will be supplied with more than enough today!

"God has Provision for His Vision!"

⌐⌐

Today's Prayer: Father thank you for your provision in my life today. Amen

INSIGHTS

Now that you have finished the first 40 days here is an opportunity to make a vow to God, one that will continue to remind you of why you are here. Vow to be a Cupbearer for the King. May you never be the same but continue to become more like him.

THE CUPBEARER'S VOW

I _____ am a Cupbearer for the King. I receive that which I also deliver that others may come to know him who is King of Kings and Lord of Lords. It is my privilege to bear the cup Christ has given me. I remember his death, burial and resurrection. I forget my past and press on toward the goal of His Kingdom, to live a life of significance with others who sojourn with me. My gifts, talents, abilities and assets are at the King's disposal and discretion for His use. My life is not my own. I vow to do my best to honor the King and His Kingdom. From this day _____forward I bear the cup, the cross and the covenant as He has sealed it with His blood, His Spirit and His word. By the presence, power and provision of the Father, Son and Holy Spirit. The Lord bless me, The Lord keep me, The Lord make His face shine upon me and be gracious to me, The Lord lift up His countenance upon me, and give me peace. Amen.

Signature _____

Final Thoughts

"I tell you, I will not drink of this fruit of the vine from now on until that day when I drink it anew with you in my Father's kingdom." When they had sung a hymn, they went out to the Mount of Olives." Matthew 26:29,30 NIV

Now that you have completed the cup challenge where are you going? Have you been inspired to change? Are you looking to start something new in your life something you have never done before? The truth is the challenge isn't over you have just started the process of a passionate lifestyle. Nothing can better define our lives than our passion for Christ. There are three things that can help in defining our passion for him. You can use them as a prayer.

- ◆ Define me, through the Cup, God help me define my purpose.

- ◆ Align me, through the Cross, God align my heart with your plan.

- ◆ Refine me, through the Covenant, God refine me through your promises.

There are many parallels to the Cup, the Cross and the Covenant you will discover. This is only the start of what I call God's Grid of Divine Grace for you to meditate on.

In the days ahead I hope you unlock a passionate lifestyle! Sing as often as you can and pray without ceasing. Take no offense and forgive quickly. Rest nightly and experience joy every morning. Love deeply and take every thought captive in your mind. Finish what you've started and start what you need to finish. As often as you break bread and drink this cup do it in remembrance of the passion of Christ and the love he has for you!

Jon Paul Tucker

About the Main Author

Jon Tucker lives with his wife Brenda and daughter Gabrielle in Haskell, Oklahoma. He is a graduate of Victory Bible Institute in Tulsa, Ok. 1985. Jon's main focus has been in the local church where he has ministered in music, taught Sunday school and ministered in many different areas. He has been writing songs since he was 16 and has always felt God's call on his life since when at the age of 17 he began to minister.

Today Jon considers his calling more defined as a Prophetic Psalmist and is writing more than ever. "I really enjoy ministering to the Lord. And if people get to sit in on it that's great to." 2007 marked a new beginning in his walk with God as he faced many challenges in his family. Then in 2008 the message on "Communion" was birthed in his heart. Along with his brother Stan they began a company and a ministry was born First Light Outreach, Inc. "I took "personal communion" for the first time on Feb. 14th, 2008 and the rest is still unfolding."

This devotional was birthed out of prayer, the word and his personal experience in God. "I hope people begin to see "Communion" in a whole new light. For me the experience has set my life on course with revelation of who he is and just how much he loves me!"

To book Jon Tucker for teaching, preaching or ministry in song you can write to:

First Light Outreach, Inc.
Rt. 2 Box 127C
Haskell, Ok. 74436

To contact by phone: 918-482-4418
Or visit the website at www.
Email address is jontucker@valornet.com

Contributing Authors

Bruce DeLay- Pastor of Heartland Church in Broken Arrow, Ok. and Radio Host
Bruce@truthinfocus.org
Day 12 "The Cup of Gethsemene" pg. 29

Bob Hill- The Coffee Guy- member of The Landing Community Church
918-321-2300
Day 18 "The Cup of Service" pg. 41

Joe Jones- Pastor of The Landing Community Church Glenpool, Ok.
Pastorjoe@thelandingonline.com or visit
www.dreams2destiny.com
Day 30 "The Cup of Dreams" pg. 67

Tony Jones- member of The Landing Community Church
Tony@ynotjesus.com or visit www.ynotjesus.com
Day 36 "The Cup of Confirmation" pg. 81

Raul Orriols- Prayer Warrior- Brother in Christ
918-321-2300
Day 8 "The Cup of Remembrance" pg. 19

Mary L. Tucker- My Mom and biggest fan
Day 34 "The Cup of Communion" pg. 77

Stan Tucker- My Brother- Pastoral Care at The Landing Community Church
Stan@thelandingonline.com
Day 39 "The Cup of Power" pg. 87

LaVergne, TN USA
06 November 2010
203829LV00003B/19/P